Gentiles and the Law
M⊘SES

Understanding Your Place As a
Gentile in God's Redemptive Plan

Ange-Michel Muhayimana

WESTBOW
PRESS®
A DIVISION OF THOMAS NELSON
& ZONDERVAN

THE HOLY BIBLE, NEW INTERNATIONAL VERSION®, NIV® Copyright © 1973, 1978, 1984, 2011 by Biblica, Inc.® Used by permission. All rights reserved worldwide. Scriptures marked KJV are taken from the KING JAMES VERSION (KJV): KING JAMES VERSION, public domain.

Scripture taken from the Amplified Bible, Copyright © 1954, 1958, 1962, 1964, 1965, 1987 by The Lockman Foundation. Used with permission.

Scripture taken from The Message. Copyright © 1993, 1994, 1995, 1996, 2000, 2001, 2002. Used by permission of NavPress Publishing Group.

WestBow Press books may be ordered through booksellers or by contacting:

WestBow Press
A Division of Thomas Nelson & Zondervan
1663 Liberty Drive
Bloomington, IN 47403
www.westbowpress.com
1 (866) 928-1240

Because of the dynamic nature of the Internet, any web addresses or links contained in this book may have changed since publication and may no longer be valid. The views expressed in this work are solely those of the author and do not necessarily reflect the views of the publisher, and the publisher hereby disclaims any responsibility for them.

Any people depicted in stock imagery provided by Thinkstock are models, and such images are being used for illustrative purposes only. Certain stock imagery © Thinkstock.

ISBN: 978-1-5127-7052-0 (sc)
ISBN: 978-1-5127-7056-8 (hc)
ISBN: 978-1-5127-7055-1 (e)

Library of Congress Control Number: 2016921467

Print information available on the last page.

WestBow Press rev. date: 12/30/2016

To my mentor René Paul Brown of Foundation Ministries International in Kerrville, Texas (U.S.A). You embraced the call of God upon your life and trained African leaders who would train their own people in return. I am a result of your obedience to the Lord. Since August 2008, you made sure I had the latest books on the gospel of grace. You invested love, time, and money in me because you obeyed what the Lord told you about me. Thank you so much!

ACKNOWLEDGMENTS

When the idea of writing this book came to my spirit, I did not know how to do it or who to turn to for help. It is an honor to have met friends who were willing to help me fulfill my childhood dream of becoming a published author.

English is my fifth language (the others are Kirundi, French, Kiswahili and Kinyarwanda), and I needed people whose first language was English.

When I met Dr. David Bramhill and his lovely wife, Sandy, we instantly connected. I was later to discover that God brought them into my life for many reasons, one of them being my editors. Thanks to the Bramhills for their tireless editing and proofreading of this manuscript. Your labor is acknowledged.

My thanks go to Mary Felde, a Norwegian missionary to Kenya. Your theological insights have helped me improve the quality of this book. I remain faithful to Jesus's finished work and to the gospel of grace. Thank you so much.

Blaise Pascal and Roselyne Matumagu, thank you for

challenging me not to give up on my dream of writing this book. I remember well how you asked members of our Tuesday Bible study fellowship to pray for me as I endeavored to become a published author. Your motivation worked.

Olivier Bigirimana and Anicet Habarugira (a.k.a Papa Rosy), thank you for hosting me when I moved to America from Burundi. Your love and hospitality will forever be engraved in my heart.

Pastor Pierre Claver Banyankiye, thank you for being a faithful disciple of Christ. I am proud to call you both my fellow servant of Christ and my son in Christ. Continue to be a good shepherd to those lovely children of God at Ekklesia. Your labor is not in vain.

Members of Ekklesia: Assembly of the Chosen, thank you for loving me as your pastor and remaining faithful to Jesus and his call upon your lives even during my absence. Yours is the crown of life.

Members of New Hope Outreach Ministries, thank you for the ten years we worked together as we traveled throughout Burundi and shared the gospel of grace with church leaders. I know this is another tool for testifying to the gospel of grace in our lovely country and beyond its borders.

To all the alumni of Amazing Grace Bible Institute and all the staff members, thank you very much for receiving the amazing good news of God's grace and love. Your questions pushed me to become the man I am today. You pushed me to study more as I strived to know Jesus. I know that most of you are sharing what we taught you in the places the Lord has taken you.

The Northminster Presbyterian Church and leadership in Tucson, Arizona, thank you for your love and support. You really live love as the Lord Jesus Christ commanded us. When I grow up, I want to be like you!

Joseph Consilivio (RIP) was greatly used in my life in regard to the relationship between Gentiles and the Law of Moses. I will always thank God for his many Facebook posts and answers when I wrote to him for a clarification about what he had posted. He is a hero of faith. I am blessed to know that I will one day meet him and tell him how I used to say that he was the apostle Paul or Jesus due to his deep insights into God's grace.

I have read many books, but when it comes to being grounded in Christ and the gospel of grace, Andrew Farley and Steve McVey have been greatly used in shaping my understanding of the finished work of Christ. I thank them for obeying God's call upon their lives because I am a result of their obedience.

Last but not least, I would like to thank my Lord Jesus Christ who saved me, loved me, and called me to serve him and his Church. His grace is the anchor of my life and ministry. This book is all about him, his grace, and his Love. I thank him for having chosen me for such a time as this. I love you because you first loved me!

ENDORSEMENTS

I knew Ange-Michel before and after grace, and I can guarantee you that the truth he shares with us in this great and wonderful book has transformed his life and made him a simple, peaceful, humble, and more lovable man. I grew up in grace through the hundreds of talks we had together. I would suggest that those who are tired and weary draw in this book the revelation that will give them rest.

—Olivier Hakizimana, evangelist and author of
What if You Aren't Who You Think?
Montreal, Canada

I call Ange-Michel Muhayimana my son because I saw him grow from the level of being a Bible student to becoming a scholar. I read *Gentiles and the Law of Moses* and liked it. I am sure it will be a blessing to many.

—Richard Otim, pastor of Rock View Baptist Church
Soroti, Uganda

Gentiles and the Law of Moses is well written, scriptural, and practical for anyone who desires to be an agent of grace and love across diverse socio-cultural and theological realities. I recommend it for nominal Bible students, theologians, and religious discourses.

—Rev. Joseph O. Obwanda, Methodist minister, excellency speaker, coach, and author of *Become Your Excellency* Nairobi, Kenya

Ange-Michel Muhayimana's *Gentiles and the Law of Moses* was the first book that awakened me to see the place of the gentiles in the Law of Moses. It helped me understand that the Law was not given to the Gentiles outside of Israel. I highly recommend it!

—Pierre-Claver Banyankiye, pastor and teacher, Ekklesia: Assemblée des Elus Bujumbura, Burundi

Ange-Michel Muhayimana's book is a masterpiece and should be considered a classic. I highly recommend it to any believer or minister who wants to be grounded in the amazing grace and love of our Lord and Savior Jesus Christ.

—Gedeon Nkeshimana, pastor of Kingdom Palace Church Bujumbura, Burundi

Ange-Michel demonstrates his gifts for Bible exposition and teaching and well as his loving pastor's heart for people to live freely in God's grace. May God use this book to set people free from the chains of legalism, to live in the abundance of a new life in Christ."

—Dr. Pete Seiferth, pastor for discipleship and multicultural ministry, Northminster Presbyterian Church
Tucson, Arizona

Ange-Michel is both an alien and a child of grace. This book is a call to live as someone who is free to live a new life of hope and peace through the spirit of liberation, given to us in Christ. I hope this book will encourage you to find your peace in our living Lord.

—Dr. Andrew Ross, senior pastor,
Northminster Presbyterian Church
Tucson, Arizona

As you read this book, you will have a clear revelation on the old and new covenant, you will be free from any spirit of religion, and you will be able to enjoy being a child of God.

—Parfait Karekezi, missionary to Rwanda, Send Me
International

I consider Angel Michel Muhayimana a friend and partner in the good news. We have spent time together in the UK and in his home of Bujumbura, Burundi. In these precious times, I have seen his gentle but determined passion to find the deeper meanings of scripture—the real heart of God for himself and for everyone around him. It has been wonderful to see the layers of revelation grow in him as he has discovered the nature of God's grace and love for mankind. In this book, he shows how this revelation has unfolded through Israel's history, specifically in relation to the Law of Moses. The rest of the world was always on God's heart, and the finished work of Jesus seals it! This work is a helpful journey for anyone seeking to understand the relationship of the Law of Moses to our condition today.

—Steve Jenkins, pastor, Life Central Church
England

CONTENTS

FOREWORD

For many years, I have struggled with how to get across the message of God's grace so that believers would understand and come out from under the Law. I find that believers everywhere suffer as they read the Old Testament with its many rules. They know in their hearts they are not entirely living up to these rules, principles, laws, and admonitions. Serious believers all over the world consider the Bible as God's Word, as infallible as his truth for us. They find it difficult to understand—if indeed it is God's truth—how it cannot apply to them. Thus, many live in condemnation though they believe in and love the Lord Jesus with all their hearts. Many see themselves as "saved" and "in Christ," yet they are plagued by guilt over "not keeping the Law."

As a teacher of the scriptures for more than thirty-five years, I have searched for ways to teach the message of grace as opposed to "living under the Law." I find the idea that we are all under the law—even those who have trusted in the finished work of Christ—is so ingrained, so deeply held, that the answer of those taught is frequently "yes, but ..." Truly the message of God's grace, the message of the finished work of Christ is such good news that it is difficult to believe. It is simply "too good to be true." It is too simple.

With so many pages of scripture (much of the Old Testament) devoted to rules, principles, laws, and admonitions, it is not easy to think it has all been set aside by the sacrifice on the cross of our Lord and Savior Jesus Christ "by abolishing in his flesh the law of commandments and ordinances" (Ephesians 2:15).

My good friend and co-laborer in Christ, Ange-Michel Muhayimana, has put in my hands his new book, *Gentiles and the Law of Moses*: *Understanding Your Place as a Gentile in God's Redemptive Plan*. It was a blessing to read the thoughts he had put down to help believers be set free in Christ. He has seen the bondage of so many Christians who simply do not understand that the Law was not given to the Gentiles; it was not God's plan of salvation for them. God had a better way in Christ, and Ange-Michel has so eloquently laid out the way that God gave his beloved family. Indeed, he states a great truth that "God wants a family." This is central to all God had planned for us. Every believer must come to see that he or she is part of this family and must relate to God by the Holy Spirit within.

Many believers simply cannot see this truth: The Bible is God's Word, God's truth, but the Lord has set aside the way of relating to him by laws and rules in favor of God's grace through faith. Ange-Michel has laid out this great truth so that everyone can see that God has given us an entirely different way to relate to him. It has nothing to do with the Law and what we do or do not do. It has everything to do with what Christ has done for us. This new way "in Christ" is totally, completely different from relating to God via the Law and rules and regulations.

Ange-Michel has set forth his premise concerning the relationship of Gentiles and the Law of God so clearly and sets about to make it easy for both Jewish believers and non-Jewish believers to understand how the Law relates (or does not relate) to present-day believers. I praise God that many who read his book and sincerely desire to hear his heart will be set free in Christ and will be able to set others free in Christ. It is so easy to read the admonitions of the apostle Paul (who many consider "the apostle of grace") and go right on not seeing how it applies to themselves.

As you read this book, try your best to open your heart and momentarily set aside what you have believed about the Law of God and Christians. Ask the Lord to open your heart and speak by his Holy Spirit to clarify everything concerning the truth of this subject. Expect a revelation of God in your spirit. The Lord is faithful and hears our cry to understand more and more of all he is trying to tell us. He wants us to understand his loving desire to relate to us directly, in truth—not based on what we do and do not do relative to law but by the Holy Spirit that lives within us.

I will never forget the day the light dawned in my life so many years ago. His grace poured into my life. It had always been there, but it took a revelation from the Lord to fully comprehend the fullness of his grace toward me. He has put in our hands a word by our brother, Ange-Michel Muhayimana, that will help in our travels toward freedom in Christ. Thank you, brother Ange-Michel.

—Rene Brown
President of Foundation Ministries International
Kerrville, Texas (U.S.A)

INTRODUCTION

In January 2009, I had an encounter with the Lord Jesus during Foundation Ministries International's outreach to the province of Ngonzi (Burundi, East Africa). At that time, I was a young man who had just graduated from Bible school in Uganda with a degree in theology and communication arts. I thought that I knew it all because of my credentials, but I was later to find out that I was wrong.

As we gathered in a tiny room coming from different provinces of Burundi, Rwanda, Uganda, Kenya, and the United States, the Lord opened my eyes to his grace. It happened as brother René Brown was teaching about God's grace and how many leaders were legalistic in their approach to the Word of God and Christianity in general. I went back to my hotel room, sat on my bed, and thought of the way I had been misleading people by teaching that believers had to live under the Law of Moses. I prayed and asked the Lord Jesus to reveal himself to me.

The following week, we returned back to Bujumbura

(the capital of Burundi), and deep in my spirit, I knew that I had started a new life in Christ. I went back to my church and started to correct lies I had been preaching (sometimes harshly or without wisdom). I began to talk more about God's grace. I had become a happy and passionate man. Life was fun! I had embarked on an eternal journey with the Lord. The journey was about learning by unlearning what I had held dearly for many years as the truth. It was the journey of learning about his love and grace.

Years went by, and I studied God's grace and organized different outreach missions, conferences, and seminars. I was on radio, television, Facebook, and other social media outlets. I taught that believers were under grace, but I did not know that the Law of Moses was never given to Gentiles.

As I taught in different countries, I encountered preachers and believers whose walks with the Lord Jesus had become nightmares. They were living under the Law of Moses as if they were in the Old Testament. I went back to the Lord and asked him to teach me about the relationship that Christians had with the Law of Moses. As I studied, I found out that many believers did not understand how Gentiles related with the Law in the Old Testament and how they are included in the church.

It is because of those questions that I felt led to write this book. I pray that, through these lines, you shall be able to know the role Moses played in the giving of the Law. You shall also know how the Israelites related to the Law and why they failed to "do" and "obey" it. You shall discover how Gentiles related to the Law in the Old Testament and how they relate to it in the New Testament by depending on what Jesus and the Holy Spirit have done. Finally, you shall discover that, because of Jesus Christ, we share the same inheritance with the Israelites—unlike under the Law of Moses in the Old Testament.

My prayer is that this book will help you to know that, as a believer, you are not under the Law of Moses. You are under grace (Romans 6:14). I pray that this book will point you to Jesus and his finished work.

May you grow in grace and in the knowledge of Jesus Christ (2 Peter 3:18).

Yours in Christ's grace,
Ange-Michel Muhayimana

CHAPTER 1

Moses and the Law

To many Christians, life is made of rules and regulations. Many of them say that they are free from the Law, but their lifestyles say something different to what they profess.

As a teacher and preacher of the Word of God, I have discovered that many Christians don't really know the purpose of the Law and the role Moses played when God gave it to him. I have also discovered that many Christians don't know the relationship that Gentiles had with the Law of Moses. Because of that ignorance, many are confused and don't live the freedom that is found in Jesus's finished work. Let's dive into the Word of God and see what it says about this important subject.

Moses the Hero

To the Israelites, Moses is a national hero who delivered them from Egyptian slavery. He established them as an independent nation, and he prepared them for an entrance into Canaan. Besides that, Moses was the man who spoke face-to-face with God; he was the man of miracles and the great lawgiver through whom Israel's worship patterns were given. Because he was a representative for his people, he received the Law from God. The Law that Moses received constituted God's covenant with the Israelites. It was God's instructions (*Torah* in Hebrew) to the Israelites on how they were to live in Canaan.

This Law worked as Israel's constitution. After being given the Law by God, Moses and the Israelites ratified the covenant (Exodus 20–24), which included the Ten Commandments, also known as the Decalogue. Concerning the ratification of the covenant, we see that after the Israelites promised to "do" and "obey" what was written in the Book of the Covenant/Law (it contained all the laws that God gave to Moses), Moses confirmed it by sprinkling blood on them as a sign of their covenant or agreement with God.

> And Moses took half of the blood, and put it in basins; and half of the blood he sprinkled on the altar. And he took the book of the Covenant, and read in the audience of the people: and they said, all that the Lord hath said we will do, and be obedient. And Moses took the blood and sprinkled it on the people, and said; behold the blood of the

> Covenant, which the Lord hath made with you concerning all these words. (Exodus 24:6–8 AMP)

When the Israelites promised to do and obey what was written in the Book of the Covenant, God knew that they would fail. As a result, he provided a system of *temporal* forgiveness through the sacrificial system and the tabernacle. The animal's blood would *cover* the sins of the person offering the sacrifice, but it could not *remove* them.

History shows us that the Mosaic Law was very difficult to do and obey to the extent that the Israelites almost gave up and were expecting a better life when the Messiah (the anointed one, or Christ) would come and deliver them from the curses caused by their disobedience to the Law (see Deuteronomy 27–28).

Even Moses the great lawgiver knew that the Israelites would disobey the Law. He also said that the Law was meant to be a witness against them. Before his death, Moses told the Israelites these words:

> Take this Book of the Law and place it beside the ark of the covenant of the Lord YOUR God. There it will remain as a witness against you. For I know how rebellious and stiff-necked you are. If you have been rebellious against the Lord while I am still alive and with you, how much more will you rebel after I die! Assemble before me all the elders

of your tribes and all your officials, so that I can speak these words in their hearing and call the heavens and the earth to testify against them. For I know that after my death you are sure to become utterly corrupt and to turn from the way I have commanded you. In days to come, disaster will fall on you because you will do evil in the sight of the Lord and arouse his anger by what your hands have made. (Deuteronomy 31:26–29 NIV)

Moses knew the people he led. He knew they were very rebellious and had stiff necks (or a selfish, obstinate, unreliable character). He knew they were utterly corrupt in their behavior and that they would turn aside from the Law. As a result, evil would befall them when he would be gone.

When Jesus was ministering in Israel's cities, towns, and synagogues, the religious leaders of his time accused him of violating the Law and looked for a way to kill him. The Pharisees, the scribes, and the Sadducees made the 613 laws a must for the Israelites; as a result, people lived in anguish and fear.

The 613 Mitzvot (Laws or Commandments)

When talking about the 613 *mitzvot* or laws, we have to understand that it is a compilation of all the laws that

God gave to Moses for the nation of Israel. The Jewish tradition teaches that there are 613 commandments. They are commonly divided into categories according to their consequences for the Israelites. There are those known as affirmative commandments and those known as negative commandments. Among them are those that apply to Israel and those that can no longer be observed because they relate to the temple, its sacrifices, and its services. We all know that the temple was destroyed in AD 70 by the Roman Empire.

The 613 laws are subdivided in groups, namely:

1. Laws talking about Yahweh (God) and how to relate with him (ten laws).
2. Laws concerning the Torah or the Law of Moses and how to treat it (six laws).
3. Laws concerning signs and symbols (five laws).
4. Laws talking about prayer and blessings (four laws).
5. Laws concerning love and brotherhood (fourteen laws).
6. Laws concerning the poor and unfortunate (thirteen laws).
7. Laws concerning the treatment of Gentiles (six laws).
8. Laws concerning marriage, divorce, and family (twenty-three laws).
9. Laws concerning forbidden sexual relations (twenty-five laws).

10. Laws concerning times and seasons (thirty-six laws).

11. Dietary laws (twenty-seven laws).

12. Laws concerning business practices (fourteen laws).

13. Laws concerning employees, servants, and slaves (nineteen laws).

14. Laws concerning vows, oaths, and swearing (seven laws).

15. Laws concerning the sabbatical and Jubilee years (seventeen laws).

16. Laws concerning the court and judicial procedure (thirty-six laws).

17. Laws concerning injuries and damages (four laws).

18. Laws concerning property and property rights (eleven laws).

19. Criminal laws (seven laws).

20. Laws concerning punishment and restitution (fourteen laws).

21. Laws concerning prophecy (three laws).

22. Laws concerning idolatry, idolaters, and idolatrous practices (forty-six laws).

23. Laws concerning agriculture and animal husbandry (seven laws).

24. Laws concerning clothing (three laws).

25. Laws concerning the firstborn (four laws).

26. Laws concerning Kohanim and Levites (thirty laws).

27. Laws concerning the *t'rumah* (heave offering), tithes, and taxes (twenty-four laws).

28. Laws concerning the temple, the sanctuary, and sacred objects (thirty-three laws).

29. Laws concerning sacrifices and offerings (112 laws).

30. Laws concerning ritual purity and impurity (sixteen laws).

31. Laws concerning lepers and leprosy (four laws).

32. Laws concerning the king (seven laws).

33. Laws concerning the Nazarites (ten laws).

34. Laws concerning wars (sixteen laws).

Despite their failure to do and obey the Law themselves, the religious leaders put a burden on the Israelites of *literally* doing and obeying all the civil, moral, and ceremonial laws (the 613 laws), thinking they would find life in them. To the latter, Jesus challenged them in these words:

> You have your heads in your Bibles constantly because you think you'll find eternal life there. But you miss the forest for the trees. These scriptures are all about me! And here I am, standing right before you, and you aren't willing to receive from me the life you say you want … But don't think I'm going to accuse you before my Father. Moses, in whom you put so much stock, is your accuser. If

you believed, really believed, what Moses said, you would believe me. *He wrote of me. If you won't take seriously what he wrote, how can I expect you to take seriously what I speak?* (John 5:39–40, 45–47 MSG, emphasis added)

I love how the Message Version puts it! The religious leaders had their heads constantly in the book of the Law, searching for life, but they could not find it. They put so much emphasis (stock) on Moses and on what he wrote and said, but they were missing the life standing in their midst. That life was Jesus Christ!

From the above verses, we see that even Jesus testified about Moses being a greater man in Israel. He testified that the Law came by Moses (John 1:17), but that *life is not found in constantly observing the Law.* Jesus showed that what Moses said and commanded spoke of him. This leads us to our next chapter, which is about the Israelites and the Law. Remember that Moses commanded the Israelites to obey the Law in its entirety. How did the Israelites relate to the Law? If they failed to obey it, what were the consequences and the solution provided by God? Follow me as we find the answers to these questions through the inspired Word of God.

CHAPTER 2

The Israelites and the
Law of Moses

Someone once said that God has always planned to have a family. In that family, God would have a loving relationship with his sons and daughters. As I pondered this truth, I remembered how God called Abraham and how he promised to bless him and his offspring (seed). Abraham's blessing was to be transferred to his biological sons, his daughters (the Israelites), and the rest of the world (Genesis 12:1–7; see also Genesis 17).

When God called Abraham, he wanted to give birth to a people who would act as a lighthouse to the nations. He wanted the Israelites to make his name known all over the world. In order to do that, God told Abraham that his descendants would be slaves to a foreign people. As the Bible tells us, Joseph was sold into slavery in Egypt to pave the way for his people. When his family finally joined him in Egypt, it was the beginning of a long walk with God for the people who would be born after them.

The Israelites in Egypt

After Joseph's death, the Israelites quickly multiplied and the Egyptians felt threatened by the Israelites' numbers. A new king who never knew Joseph came to power and made plans to destroy the Israelites.

> Now Joseph and all his brothers and all that generation died, but the Israelites were fruitful and multiplied greatly and became exceedingly numerous, so that the land was filled with them. Then a new king, who did not know about Joseph, came to power in Egypt. "Look" he said to his people, "The Israelites have become much too numerous for us. Come, we must deal shrewdly with them or they will become even more numerous and, if war breaks out, will join our enemies, fight against us and leave the country." So they put slave masters over them to oppress them with forced labor … But the more they were oppressed, the more they multiplied and spread; so the Egyptians came to dread the Israelites and worked them ruthlessly. (Exodus 1:6–13 NIV)

It was because of this misery that God decided to call Moses, who was raised by Pharaoh's daughter, to rescue his people from Egypt. Concerning the Israelites' misery and oppression in Egypt, God clarified Moses's mission.

> I have indeed seen the misery of my people in Egypt. I have heard them crying out because of their slave drivers, and I am concerned about their suffering. So I have come down to rescue them from the hand of the Egyptians and to bring them up out of that land into a good and spacious land, a land flowing with milk and honey … And now the cry of the Israelites has reached me, and I have seen the way the Egyptians are oppressing them. So now, go. I am sending you to pharaoh to bring my people the Israelites out of Egypt. (Exodus 3:7–10 NIV)

This conversation between God and Moses was to usher in a new era for the Israelites. It was an era of walking with God, an era of walking in freedom and miracles. It was an era of relying on God and what he would do for them.

The Israelites and the Law

It has always amazed me to see how God rescued the Israelites with miraculous works—and still they rebelled against him and almost returned to Egypt.

When God led the Israelites out of Egypt, he used Moses as a mediator. Because the Israelites did not know God, they asked Moses who he was and how he was called. At the burning bush, Moses asked God's name (Exodus 3:13). To Moses's request, God told him that his name is "I Am." God said, "I Am who I Am" (Exodus 3:13–14 NIV).

God wanted Moses to know that he is the Everlasting One—the God who is not limited by time. He wanted Moses and the Israelites to know that he is the same yesterday, today, and forever (Hebrews 13:8). In summary, he wanted them to know that he is the Unchanging God, the God of Abraham, Isaac, and Jacob (Exodus 3:15).

God has always wanted to have a family of sons and daughters. He has always wanted to have a loving relationship with human beings. In the case of the Israelites, God led them out of Egypt because he wanted a people for himself (Exodus 19:4). Therefore, God asked Moses to go to the top of Mount Sinai to meet with him so that he would continue to make himself known to the Israelites. Remember that the Israelites had seen him perform miracles in Pharaoh's house by sending plagues all over Egypt, crossing the Red Sea, and performing many other miracles. He did all that because he wanted them to know him more.

As the Israelites settled at Mount Sinai (in the Desert of Sinai) after three months of walking, God summoned Moses to join him at the top. There, God spoke to Moses and

Aaron while the Israelites remained at a distance (Exodus 20:21). That was when God gave them the Law. When God gave them the Law, the Israelites responded with one voice, "Everything the Lord has said we will do" (Exodus 24:3 NIV). After this, Moses went on to ratify God's covenant of the Law with the Israelites (Exodus 24:6–8).

After the ratification of the Covenant, the Israelites for the first time lived under the Mosaic Law. Because God knew that the Israelites would fail to fulfill all the laws (civil, moral, and ceremonial) given to them, he made a special provision in the system of the Tabernacle.

After giving the Law to Moses and the Israelites, he told Moses to build a movable tent in which they were to sacrifice animals after they had sinned (Exodus 25–30). The animals' blood was to *cover* the sins of the sinner, and each year, the high priest who acted as a representative of the Israelites before God would enter the holy of holies with blood to sprinkle it on the mercy seat which was on top of the Ark of the Covenant (Leviticus 16:21; Hebrews 10:1–3). *This was done as a reminder of sins.*

> The Law is only a shadow of the good things that are coming—not the realities themselves. For this reason, it can never, by the same sacrifices repeated endlessly year after year, make perfect those who draw near to worship. If it could, would they not

have stopped being offered? For the worshipers would have been cleansed once for all, and would no longer have felt guilty for their sins. But those sacrifices are an annual reminder of sins, because it is impossible for the blood of bulls and goats to take away sins. (Hebrews 10:1–3 NIV)

From the above verses, we see that:

- The Law was a shadow of the good things to come.
- The Law could not make the Israelites perfect.
- The Law made the Israelites feel guilty for their sins.
- The sacrifices were an annual reminder of sins.
- The blood of animals could not take away sins

As we shall see in the coming chapter, Jesus came to fulfill what the Israelites longed for according to this verse. That is why throughout the Old Testament, we see that the Israelites almost always turned their backs on God and his Law because it was *impossible* to *literally* fulfill.

CHAPTER 3

Gentiles and the Law of Moses

In the previous two chapters, we saw that Moses was a mediator between God and the Israelites. We saw that it was through him that the Law came. We also saw that the Israelites promised that they would "do" and "obey" everything that was written in the book of the Law, yet they failed.

The question that might be popping up in your mind right now as you read through these lines is: *What was the Gentiles' relationship to the Mosaic Law?* I want to assure you that you are not alone to ask that question. I asked myself that same question for many years, but I could not get a clear answer to it. I also believe that many Christians around the world still don't know how Gentiles related with the Law and what the Bible has to say about it. I hope that this chapter will open your eyes about how Gentiles relate with the Law and how you can be freed from religious duties that you may be basing your Christian life on.

Who is a Gentile?

Before going any further with this chapter, I find it very important to define the word *Gentile*. When the Bible talks about Gentiles, it is talking about non-Israelite people. We have to remember that the Israelites are the biological descendants of Abraham, Isaac, and Jacob whom God later called Israel.

The Hebrew word for *"Gentile"* is *Gôy*, and the Greek word for *Gentiles* is *Ethnos*. The two words translate as a *people* or *nations*. In this context, they mean a non-Israelite people. That is why the Israelites put a distinction between themselves and other nations that did not descend from Jacob (Israel).

Gentiles' Place in Israel

When God called Abram (who was later called Abraham), he had a vision of blessing the whole world through him. In Genesis 12, we see God's plan in these words:

> The Lord had said to Abram, "Leave your country, your people and your father's household and go to the land I will show you. I will make you into a great nation and I will bless you; I will make your name great, and you will be a blessing ... and all

peoples on earth will be blessed through you."
(Genesis 12:1–3 NIV)

In the above verses, we see that God had a plan for blessing the nation of Israel, and that he also had a plan for blessing the other nations through Abraham. We can see that every person of every time has access to the promise of Abraham and can appropriate it for himself or herself.

Abraham's promise fulfilled in Christ

Paul the great apostle to the Gentiles understood that Jesus could be found throughout the Old Testament in prophecies, images, and events foreshadowing his life, death, and resurrection. In the case of God's promise to Abraham of blessing all peoples on earth through him, Paul clearly shows that that promise was fulfilled in Christ.

> Consider Abraham: "He believed God, and it was credited to him as righteousness." Understand, then, that those who believe are children of Abraham. The Scripture foresaw that God would justify the Gentiles by faith, and announced the gospel in advance to Abraham: "All nations will be blessed through you." So those who have faith are blessed along with Abraham, the man of faith. (Galatians 3:6–9 NIV)

In his omniscience, God knew what he had planned for the Gentiles. He called Abraham and promised to make him a blessing to the whole world. In the passage above, we see that he wanted to justify (to make righteous) the Gentiles by faith, but not by the Law because the law is not of faith (Galatians 3:12).

During Jesus's ministry—and even before him—the Israelites took pride in the fact that they were the only children of Abraham. Gentiles and Israelites are both children of God because of their faith in Jesus. Paul says that those who believe are the true children of Abraham (Galatians 3:6). He does not say that those who are under the Law of Moses are the only children of Abraham. That was true under the era of the Law of Moses. Today, in the era of the church, *only* those Jews and Gentiles who have believed in Jesus as their personal Savior, Lord, and life are considered to be the legitimate children of Abraham. If you are in Christ by faith, you are Abraham's son or daughter. You are a partaker of the Abrahamic blessing. You are already blessed!

The Holy Spirit is the Abrahamic blessing.

For many years, I believed that the blessing spoken about in Genesis 12 and 17 was financial or material because of the so-called prosperity gospel (which is no gospel at all). I used to ask myself why I was not seeing the dollars in my bank account if I was a partaker of the Abrahamic blessing. As a result to that faulty belief, I felt guilty because I believed that I had little faith to merit such an amazing blessing. I resolved to study hard, pray more, confess hard, and fast as many times as I could in order to earn or merit God's blessing(s). I praise God because the Holy Spirit revealed to me that I am not blessed in terms of money, houses, or any other material things the world offers; the Holy Spirit's presence in my life is the blessing being talked about in Genesis 12. Paul explains it in these words:

> He redeemed us in order that the blessing given to Abraham might come to the Gentiles through Christ Jesus, so that by faith we might receive the promise of the Spirit. (Galatians 3:14 NIV)

The blessing being spoken about is the Holy Spirit. God wanted the Holy Spirit (the blessing) to come to the Gentiles through Jesus Christ. That is why Jews and Gentiles are saved by grace through faith (Ephesians 2:8–10). He wanted the Gentiles to be justified by faith in Jesus Christ. We have to remember that—just as we received the Holy Spirit by faith—we are also justified by faith without any intervention of the Law of Moses.

Jesus as the Seed/Offspring of Abraham

The Bible clearly shows us that God has always planned to bless the world through Jesus Christ. To do so, he chose a man called Abram whose name was changed into Abraham because he was to be a father of many nations/multitudes (see Genesis 17:4–5). By giving him this promise, God accompanied it with one of the greatest promises found in the Bible. It is the promise of blessing the world through Abraham's offspring or seed.

> The Lord appeared to Abram and said, "To your offspring I will give this land." So he built an altar there to the Lord, who had appeared to him. (Genesis 12:7 NIV)

After doing some study, I found out that the word *offspring* in Hebrew is the word *Zera* from the root word *Zara*. That word has many meanings: *to plant, seed, grain, crop, descendants, family, race,* and *semen.* While doing further studies on the meaning of the word *Zera,* I found out that it is used in Genesis 3:15 in the singular. The word *offspring* refers to Jesus Christ. We have to remember that the first promise of Christ in the Bible is announced by God to Adam in Genesis 3:15. It was enlarged by the Abrahamic covenant in Genesis 12:7, made specific in David's lineage in 2 Samuel 7:12, and realized in Jesus Christ as Paul clarified it.

> Brothers, let me take an example from everyday life. Just as no one can set aside or add to a human covenant that has been duly established, so it is in this case. The promises were spoken to Abraham and to his seed. The Scripture does not say "and to seeds," meaning many people, but "and to your seed," meaning one person, who is Christ. What I mean is this: The law, introduced 430 years later, does not set aside the covenant previously established by God and thus do away with the promise. For if the inheritance depends on the law, then it no longer depends on a promise; but God in his grace gave it to Abraham through a promise. (Galatians 3:15–18 NIV)

God, in his foreknowledge, wanted the Gentiles to be blessed in Jesus Christ. The seed promised to Abraham as the source of the world's blessing was Jesus. That is why the Bible says that those who believe in Jesus are Abraham's sons and daughters. We are not God's children because of the Law of Moses. We have not received the inheritance or promise (the Holy Spirit) by the Law of Moses. The Law was introduced 430 years after the promise was given to Abraham (Galatians 3:18). God wanted the whole world (Gentiles and Jews) to be blessed together in Jesus Christ, but Gentiles were not going to be under the Law. That is why it is paramount to understand how Gentiles living in Israel were called and how they were to relate to the Law of Moses.

The Proselytes

The Bible teaches that there are two categories of Gentiles. There are those known as the proselytes and general Gentiles or those living outside of Israel. So who is a proselyte? According to *Easton's Bible Dictionary*, a proselyte is a "stranger" (1 Chronicles 22:2), a comer to Palestine, and a "sojourner in the land" (Exodus 12:48; 20:10; 22:21). In the New Testament, a proselyte is a "convert to Judaism."

The Bible records two groups or categories of proselytes. There are those known as "proselytes of the gate" (Exodus 20:8–9) and "proselytes of righteousness/devout men/men fearing God/men worshipping God/converts to Judaism."

The *Easton's Bible Dictionary* explains the distinction between these two categories comprising the proselytes in these words:

> The distinction between "proselytes of the gate" (Exodus 20:10) and "proselytes of righteousness" originated only with the rabbis. According to them, the "proselytes of the gate" (half proselytes) were not required to be circumcised nor to comply with the Mosaic ceremonial law. They were bound

only to conform to the so-called seven precepts of Noah, viz., to abstain from idolatry, blasphemy, bloodshed, uncleanness, the eating of blood, theft, and to yield obedience to the authorities. Besides these laws, however, they were required to abstain from work on the Sabbath, and to refrain from the use of leavened bread during the time of the Passover. The "proselytes of righteousness, " religious or devout proselytes (Acts 13:43), were bound to all the doctrines and precepts of the Jewish economy, and were members of the synagogue in full communion. The name "proselyte" occurs in the New Testament only in Matthew 23:15 and Acts 2:10; 6:5; 13:43. The name by which they are commonly designated is that of "devout men," or men "fearing God" or "worshipping God."

This clarification will help us to put a distinction between Gentiles who lived in Israel and those who lived in other kingdoms (nations) of the world. It will also help us in getting a better understanding of how Jews and Gentiles are blessed together in Christ without any intervention of the Law of Moses.

The Inclusion of Gentiles in God's Redemptive Plan

As we saw in the previous paragraphs, there were Gentiles known as proselytes who lived in Israel and Gentiles who lived outside Israel. This means that the Gentiles' *inclusion* in God's covenant of the Law is a sign that it was a shadow of how the whole Gentile world would be grafted in Christ by grace through faith. Concerning the inclusion of the Gentiles in the Old Covenant, Isaiah said,

> Foreigners who bind themselves to the Lord to serve him, to love the name of the Lord, and to worship him, all who keep the Sabbath without desecrating it and who hold fast to my covenant-these I will bring to my holy mountain and give them joy in my house of prayer. Their burnt offerings and sacrifices will be accepted on my altar; for my house will be called a house of prayer for all nations. The Sovereign Lord declares—he who gathers the exiles of Israel: "I will gather still others to them besides those already gathered. (Isaiah 56:6–8 NIV)

This shows us that non-Israelites who decided to bind themselves to hold to God's covenant of the Law would be given a place among God's chosen people (the Israelites). We have to understand that this did not make them into

Israelites as many think. They remained Gentiles with a special place among God's people because they had decided to know God, worship him, and bind themselves to his Law or covenant.

Many examples of God's inclusion of the Gentiles in his redemptive plan can be found in the Bible. People like Rahab the prostitute, Ruth, Bathsheba, and many others in Jesus's genealogy were Gentiles whom God included in his redemptive plan not because of what they did but because of his unmerited favor (grace). What about the Ninivites? The Ninivites, according to the Bible, were a cruel people, but because God wanted the nation of Israel to play her role of a *missionary nation*, he sent Jonah to tell them to repent from their wickedness. We have to remember that *God chose Israel as the center for world evangelization.* He sent Jonah to the Ninivites to make them know the true God and his moral character. When Jonah preached to them about God and what he wanted them to do, they repented and worshiped him. Did they keep his laws? They did for a short while, but then they fell back again into their idolatrous ways.

I one time had a discussion with a fellow minister who contended that the Gentiles were given the Law of Moses because the Israelites went out and preached to them. When I told him that some of the Gentiles living outside of Israel were taught to obey God, but were never given the Law, he could not believe it. He said that Israel had a missionary vocation (which I agree with) of making the Gentiles live under the Law. I told him that, according to the teaching of the Bible, the Gentiles were never given the Law of Moses. It was given to the nation of Israel, but it included Gentiles who decided to live in Israel or bind themselves to the Jewish faith. They were to live by the same rules and regulations as the Israelites if they chose to live like them.

The Exclusion of Gentiles from Israel

Even if Gentiles were included in God's redemptive plan, the Bible teaches that *they were excluded to a certain extent*. God made sure the nation of Israel understood that they were different to other nations (Gentiles):

> Keep all my decrees and laws and follow them, so that the land where I am bringing you to live may not vomit you out. You must not live according to the customs of the nations I am going to drive out before you. Because they did all these things, I abhorred them.
>
> But I said to you, "You will possess their land; I will give it to you as an inheritance, a land flowing with milk and honey. I am the Lord your God, who has set you apart from the nations.

You must therefore make a distinction between clean and unclean animals and between unclean and clean birds. Do not defile yourselves by any animal or bird or anything that moves along the ground—those which I have set apart as unclean for you.

You are to be holy to me because I, the Lord, am holy, and I have set you apart from the nations to be my own." (Leviticus 20:22–26 NIV)

Why did God set apart the nation of Israel? It was because God wanted them to become a light to the Gentiles. He wanted them to be his own possession among other nations.

It is too small a thing for you to be my servant to restore the tribes of Jacob and bring back those of Israel I have kept. I will also make you a light for the Gentiles, which you may bring my salvation to the ends of the earth. (Isaiah 49:6 NIV)

The above verses clearly show us that there was a difference between the Israelites and other nations (Gentiles). Isaiah 49:6 is a prophetic verse about Jesus's mission on earth. The verse still shows that Gentiles were in the darkness because they did not know anything about God and his Law. Now let us see how the Gentiles related to the Law of Moses and how the Israelites were to treat them according to the Law.

The Gentiles and the Law of Moses in the Old Covenant

When God gave the Law to Moses, he also told him how it was to be used, its purpose and how foreigners or Gentiles (proselytes) who lived among them were to be treated. The laws given to the Israelites were also meant to turn the world's attention toward God.

> But all of you who held fast to the Lord your God are still alive today. See, I have taught you decrees and laws the Lord my God commanded me, so that you may follow them in the land you are entering to take possession of it. Observe them carefully, for this will show your wisdom and understanding to the nations, who will hear about all these decrees and say, "Surely this great nation is a wise and understanding people." What other nation is so great as to have their gods near them the way the Lord our God is near us whenever we pray to him? And what other nation is so great as to have such righteous decrees and laws as this body of laws I am setting before you today? (Deuteronomy 4:6 NIV)

Through the Law, God showed that he loved and provided for the Gentiles:

> For the Lord your God is God of gods and Lord of lords, the great God, mighty and awesome, who shows no partiality and accepts no bribes. He defends the cause of the fatherless and the widow, and loves the alien, giving him food and clothing. (Deuteronomy 10:18 NIV)

> When you reap the harvest of your land, do not reap to the very edges of your field or gather the gleanings of your harvest. Leave them for the poor and the alien. I am the Lord your God. (Leviticus 23:22 NIV)

Through the Law, God ordained the Israelites to love foreigners as themselves:

> When an alien lives with you in your land, do not mistreat him. The alien living with you must be treated as one of your native-born. Love him as yourself, for you were aliens in Egypt. I am the Lord your God. (Leviticus 19:33–34 NIV)

> Do not oppress an alien; you yourselves know how it feels to be aliens, because you were aliens in Egypt/ (Exodus 23:9 NIV).

Under the Law, the Israelites and the Gentiles (aliens) who lived in Israel were to be equally treated:

> The community is to have the same rules for you and for the alien living among you; this is a lasting ordinance for the generations to come. You and the alien shall be the same before the Lord: The same laws and regulations will apply both to you and to the alien living among you. (Numbers 15:15–16 NIV)

We have to note that this only applied to those Gentiles living in Israel. It did not apply to those living outside the land of Israel unless they chose to bind themselves to God's covenant and to the Jewish customs.

Gentiles (proselytes) living in Israel who wanted to celebrate the Passover had to have all the males in their households circumcised and were to be treated like one born in the land (an Israelite):

> An alien living among you who wants to celebrate the Lord's Passover must have all the males in his household circumcised; then he may take part like one born in the land. No uncircumcised male may eat of it. The same law applies to the native-born and to the alien living among you. (Exodus 12:48–49 NIV)

The above verses show us how God is impartial and loving. He made sure the Israelites did not mistreat the aliens living among them. He reminded them that they also used to be aliens in Egypt, which was why they were to be different to their former oppressors by showing love and hospitality to foreigners living among them. This attitude speaks to us today. Many of you know people who migrated or are refugees in your motherland. How do you treat them? Do you oppress them? Do you consider them as second-class citizens? Your answers to these questions will reveal how deep your understanding of God's love and hospitality is.

To what laws were Gentiles outside Israel accountable?

As a Bible teacher and preacher, I have encountered numerous preachers, teachers, and Christians who cannot answer this question. When you listen to many prominent teachers and preachers talking about the Gentiles' relationship to the Law, you might think that the Law of Moses was also given to the whole world. This way of teaching is not at all scriptural. We must be able to teach what the Bible teaches. The Bible does not teach that the Gentiles outside of Israel were given the Law of Moses. If they were not under the Mosaic Law, to which law were they accountable?

The Patriarchal Laws

When I was doing some research and study on this subject, I was amazed when I discovered that, prior to the Law of Moses, there were other laws that God gave to the Patriarchs like Noah, Abraham (Genesis 26:5), Job, and other heads of families in different nations. Wayne Jackson explains:

> Prior to the giving of the Mosaic Law, the whole world was under what is commonly called Patriarchal law. The father of each household was the family "priest," so to speak. He led the worship by the offering of sacrifices to God. The Lord communicated directly with the people in various ways, e.g. by dreams (Gen. 31:11), visions (Gen. 46:2), personal appearances (Gen. 18:1), and specially appointed emissaries like Melchizedek (see Gen. 14:1ff; cf. also Heb. 1:1). The patriarchal worship system is well illustrated in the lives of such men as Job (cf. 1:5) and Abraham (Gen. 12:8; 13:4, etc.). One historian has observed: "The concept of the patriarchal 'God of the fathers' is paralleled from the Old Assyrian tablets of the 19th century B. C. found in Cappacodia" (Yamauchi, 1290). When the Hebrews were segregated from the balance of humanity, as a "holy people" for Jehovah's "own

possession" (Dt. 7:6; 14:2), the Gentiles continued under the Patriarchal system until they were offered the gospel, and the Patriarchal regime was replaced by the international Christian system (Acts 10). Romans 1:18ff shows how those ancient Gentiles were accountable to God for their beliefs and conduct. Romans 2:12–16 amplifies the point by suggesting that even the patriarchs, who had no written revelation from the Lord, possessed a threshold sense of the difference between right and wrong (called "conscience"), and when they rejected the former and embraced the latter, they stood condemned. When the Gentiles sinned (and there can be no sin without law—Romans 4:15; 1 John 3:4), they were punished. Ultimately, those antique nations will be judged by the "light" which they possessed, and not by that which is available today through the Scriptures. We are under a significantly greater measure of accountability in this age. At times, certain Gentiles would join themselves to the Hebrews by means of the "proselyte" procedure. On the day of Pentecost there were assembled at Jerusalem both "Jews and proselytes" (Acts 2:11; cf. 6:5; 13:43). This meant that male Gentiles would receive circumcision, and all of the "converts" to the Israelite system would accept the responsibilities of the Mosaic Law. There was even a place in the temple (called the Court of the Gentiles) to accommodate these adherents to Judaism.

We can see that the Gentiles outside Israel lived under another type of law, which was different from the Mosaic Law. The patriarchal law put in the Gentiles' consciences a sense of knowing the wrong from the good (see the tree of the knowledge of good and evil). That is why teaching that the Gentiles outside Israel had the Mosaic Law is a heresy. We must also understand that God put a *conscience* in any person for self-critique when we do right or wrong. This is still applicable today—until one receives the gift of the Holy Spirit and is led by him. Does it mean that the unbelievers who heard the gospel and rejected it will be judged by their consciences? No. God will judge people depending on their faith in Jesus Christ or their unbelief in him. That is why the Bible teaches that the Gospel of the kingdom of God shall be preached in the whole world as a testimony or sign to all nations that the end will come (Matthew 24:14). When Jesus comes back, the whole gospel will have reached the whole world so that people will be judged according to their cultures, consciences, and relationships with Jesus Christ.

Some verses prove that the Gentiles living outside of Israel were not given the Mosaic Law. It is important to clarify what the Bible says about how the Gentiles outside of Israel lived without the Mosaic Law. A number of verses enable us to see that the Law of Moses was never given to any other nation. Understanding this truth will free you from religious beliefs and make you love God more than ever before because you will see how much God has loved you and adopted you in his family (the church, which includes Gentiles and Israelites) if you are a non-Israelite (Gentile). Let's dive into the Bible and see what it says on this matter.

The Law was not given to the Gentiles.

> He has revealed his word to Jacob, his laws and decrees to Israel. He has done this for no other nation; they do not know his laws. Praise the Lord. (Psalm 147:19–20 NIV)

As we can see in this verse, God never gave the Law to the Gentiles. No other nation knew Moses's Law except Israel. That is why teaching that the Law of Moses was applicable to the whole world is a false teaching, which we must address in the body of Christ. If you are reading this and find that you have been teaching that the Law was given to the Gentiles, go back to your congregation and tell them the truth so that they may walk in freedom.

The Law of Moses put a separation between the Israelites and the Gentiles.

Therefore, remember that formerly you who are Gentiles by birth and called "uncircumcised" by those who call themselves "the circumcision" (that done in the body by the hands of men) Remember that at that time you were separate from Christ, excluded from citizenship in Israel and foreigners to the covenants of the promise, without hope and without God in the world. (Ephesians 2:11–12 NIV)

Understanding that the Law of Moses put a separation between the Gentiles and the Israelites is key to knowing how to apply the Law. We have to understand that the Law excluded the Gentiles from the Israelites to the extent that the latter could not have any relationship with the former because they were thought to be unclean or defiled (see Peter's vision in Acts 10:13–25).

The Bible also shows us that the Jews could not share a meal with the Gentiles.

When Peter came to Antioch, I opposed him to his face, because he was clearly in the wrong. Before certain men came from James, he used to eat with the Gentiles. But when they arrived, he began to draw back and separate himself from the Gentiles because he was afraid of those who belonged to the circumcision group. (Galatians 2:11–22 NIV)

God's Law, covenants, and promises were exclusively for the Israelites, but not for the Gentiles.

> I am speaking the truth in Christ. I am not lying; my conscience [enlightened and prompted] by the Holy Spirit bearing witness with me that I have bitter grief and incessant anguish in my heart. For I could wish that I myself were accursed and cut off and banished from Christ for the sake of my brethren and instead of them, my natural kinsmen and my fellow countrymen. For they are Israelites, and to them belong God's adoption [as a nation] and the glorious presence (Shekinah). With them were the special covenants made, to them was the Law given. To them [the temple] worship was revealed and [God's own] promises announced. To them belong the patriarchs, and as far as his natural descent was concerned, from them is the Christ, who is exalted and supreme over all, God, blessed forever! Amen (so let it be). (Romans 9:1–5 The Amplified Bible)

By studying these verses, I was able to get seven important truths, which I think are very helpful for understanding how Gentiles were not given the Law of Moses.

1. Israelites are different to Gentiles.

2. God adopted Israel as a nation. No other nation is said to be set apart by God and for God. God's glorious presence first belonged to the Israelites (but not to the Gentiles).

3. God's special covenants were made to the Israelites (but not to the Gentiles).

4. God's Law was given to the Israelites (but not to the Gentiles).

5. The Temple worship was given to the Israelites (but not to the Gentiles).

6. God's promises were directly given to the Israelites (but not to the Gentiles).

When these truths are compared to each other, we are able to get a clearer understanding of why Paul always put a distinction between the Israelites and the Gentiles.

> Therefore, remember that formerly you who are Gentiles by birth and called "uncircumcised" by those who call themselves "the circumcision" (that done in the body by the hands of men) remember that at that time you were separate from Christ, excluded from citizenship in Israel and foreigners to the covenants of the promise, without hope and without God in the world. But now in Christ Jesus you who once were far away have been brought

near through the blood of Christ. (Ephesians 2:11–13 NIV)

Many preachers and teachers say that Gentiles were—and are still—under the Law of Moses, but we can see from the above verses that:

1. By birth, Gentiles were different to the Israelites.
2. Israelites called the Gentiles the "uncircumcised" because circumcision was the physical sign of belonging to God for the Israelites. That is why Gentiles living in Israel had to be circumcised for them to take part in the Passover. However, Gentiles outside of Israel could not be under any of the Mosaic Laws because they were not living in the land of Israel.
3. Gentiles were separate from Christ or the Messiah. That is because Christ, according to the Law and the prophets, was to come especially for the Israelites and then for the Gentiles (we shall see this later in this chapter).
4. Gentiles were excluded from citizenship in Israel. This means that Gentiles were not allowed to be citizens in Israel unless they came to live in Israel and bound themselves to the Law of Moses (as we saw earlier).
5. Gentiles were foreigners to the promise of the covenants. This means that the different covenants

talked about in the Bible (Abrahamic, Noahic, Mosaic, and Davidic) were mainly directed to the Israelites. That is why, as we shall see later, Gentiles were considered second-class people by the Israelites.

6. Gentiles were without hope because they did not know anything about Christ's coming to save the world. They worshiped false gods that could never save them from sin, death, and eternal damnation.

7. Gentiles were without God in the world because they were not connected to any of his covenants and promises. This means that Gentiles did not have fellowship with God. We all know that God is a God of the whole world; however, he made himself known to the Israelites in spite of other nations.

As you can see, Gentiles were *included* in God's eternal plan of saving the world through Jesus Christ, but they were also *excluded* from citizenship in Israel. God did not give them the Law of Moses. *He never expected them to live under it unless they chose to.* In order to understand how Gentiles were not given the Law of Moses, let's see how Jesus related with them during his earthly ministry.

Jesus and the Gentiles

When I was still an itinerant minister, I used to encounter Muslims who would oppose my ministry partners and me by asking us tricky questions that seemed difficult. They would tell us that the Bible says that Jesus did not come for other nations. They would show us in the Bible that salvation belonged to Israel alone. Because I was not knowledgeable in what I know now, I would get confused in front of the people that I led. I would be speechless and defeated. However, those challenges pushed me to study even more so that I could discover what the Bible said about it.

I know that some of you have gone through this same experience. Maybe some of you have decided to give up on Christianity by thinking that God did not send Jesus to save you because you are not an Israelite. You might be confused because nobody is able to give you the answers you have been looking for. If you are in this category, I want to assure you that there is an answer for you. Do not put this book down! Keep reading and discover for yourself how Jesus first came for Israel and then included the Gentiles. The truth hidden behind how Jesus related with the Gentiles is going to set you free from religious bondage and fear.

Simeon said that Jesus was a light for revelation to the Gentiles and for glory to God's people Israel.

Now there was a man in Jerusalem called Simeon, who was righteous and devout. He was waiting for the consolation of Israel, and the Holy Spirit was upon him.

It had been revealed to him by the Holy Spirit that he would not die before he had seen the Lord's Christ. Moved by the Spirit, he went into the temple courts. When the parents brought in the child Jesus to do for him what the custom of the Law required, Simeon took him in his arms and praised God, saying: "Sovereign Lord, as you have promised, you now dismiss your servant in peace. For my eyes have seen your salvation, which you have prepared in the sight of all people, a light for revelation to the Gentiles and for glory to your people Israel." (Luke 2:25–32 NIV)

You can see that even Simeon understood the distinction between Gentiles and the Israelites. He also understood how Jesus was to relate with both groups of people.

Isaiah prophesied that Jesus would show judgment to the Gentiles and that they would trust in his name. This means that Jesus was to teach Gentiles God's ways and that they would believe (trust) in his name to be saved.

But when Jesus knew it, he withdrew himself from thence: and great multitudes followed him, and he healed them all; And charged them that they should not make him known: That it might be fulfilled which was spoken by Esaias the prophet, saying, behold my servant, whom I have chosen; my beloved, in whom my soul is well pleased: I will put my spirit upon him, and he shall show judgment to the Gentiles. He shall not strive, nor cry; neither shall any man hear his voice in the streets. A bruised reed shall he not break, and smoking flax shall he not quench, till he sends forth judgment unto victory. And in his name shall the Gentiles trust. (Matthew 12:15–21 KJV)

Jesus urged the Israelites not to be anxious over life's needs (as the Gentiles were).

Therefore, take no thought, saying, what shall we eat? Or, what shall we drink? Or, Wherewithal shall we be clothed? (For after all these things do the Gentiles seek) for your heavenly Father knoweth that ye have need of all these things. (Mathew 6:30–32 KJV)

When Jesus was saying these words, he wanted the Israelites to remember that God was their Father and that he cared for them as his chosen people. He wanted to remind them that according to the Law, they were different from the Gentiles who were aliens to God's promises.

When Jesus sent his twelve disciples to go preach the good news of the kingdom, he forbade them to go among the Gentiles or enter any town of the Samaritans. He asked them to go to the lost sheep of Israel.

> He called his twelve disciples to him and gave them authority to drive out evil spirits and to heal every disease and sickness ... These twelve Jesus sent out with the following instructions: "Do not go among the Gentiles or enter any town of the Samaritans. Go rather to the lost sheep of Israel." (Mathew 10:1–6 NIV)

Since I was never taught the difference between Israelites and Gentiles—and how they became one in Christ—I was confused and saw the Bible as full of errors. I also got angry with God because I was convinced that he only saved the Israelites and rejected the Gentiles (including me).

In January 2009, God revealed the gospel of grace to me. I started to see that Gentiles were also included in God's eternal plan of salvation in Christ. I learned that when Jesus was forbidding his disciples to go to the Gentiles or to any town of the Samaritans (Samaritans were a mixture of

Gentiles and Israelites), it was because he wanted to fulfill what God had started with the nation of Israel. Remember that Israel was chosen among other nations to be God's light to the world. *Israel was to carry the gospel to the rest of the world.* That is why they were to go first to the lost sheep of Israel and proclaim the good news of the kingdom because the Messiah who was to restore the Kingdom to Israel had come. Remember that God's promises and covenants belong to Israel.

Jesus said that he was sent only to the lost sheep of Israel:

> Leaving that place, Jesus withdrew to the region of Tyre and Sidon. A Canaanite woman from that vicinity came to him, crying out, "Lord, Son of David, have mercy on me! My daughter is suffering terribly from demon-possession." Jesus did not answer a word. So his disciples came to him and urged him, "Send her away, for she keeps crying out after us." He answered, "I was sent only to the lost sheep of Israel. "The woman came and knelt before him. "Lord, help me!" she said.
>
> He replied, "It is not right to take the children's bread and toss it to their dogs." "Yes, Lord," she said, "but even the dogs eat the crumbs that fall from their masters' table." Then Jesus answered, "Woman, you have great faith! Your request is

granted." And her daughter was healed from that very hour. (Mathew 15:21–18 NIV)

From these verses, we see that Jesus confirms that he was only sent to the lost sheep of Israel. What about the Gentiles? We saw that Isaiah prophesied that Gentiles would trust in his name and be saved. But how were they going to be saved if he was not sent to them?

We have to understand that when Jesus was sent to the lost sheep of Israel, he wanted them to first believe in him so that they might take the gospel to the Gentiles, which they did after Pentecost. We have to see that among the people who were filled by the Holy Spirit on Pentecost, there was not even one Gentile. All were Israelites. It has always been Israel's call to make God known among the Gentiles.

Note also that Jesus calls the Gentiles "dogs." He also says that it was not right to take the children's bread and toss it to their "dogs."

The bread Jesus is talking about is God's promise of salvation given to Israel. Remember that Gentiles were foreigners to God's covenants and promises. That is why they were considered dogs, which eat leftovers.

We shall see how Gentiles were included by grace in God's eternal plan of saving the world through Christ. Knowing this completely changed the way I see God, myself, and life in general. It made me be grateful to God for having included me in Christ as a Gentile because he chose to do so by his grace.

Jesus as the last Adam included Gentiles in his crucifixion.

Bible students know that Adam means *humanity* or the *human race*. It is in that perspective that Jesus came as the last Adam or the head of the human race. He identified himself with the first Adam in order to save those who were born after him (the first Adam). He came as the last Adam to usher in a new human race known as new creatures (2 Corinthians 5:17).

Jesus as the last Adam took Adam's failure on himself and crucified humanity (Gentiles and Israelites) in his body. *We have to note that the first Adam was not an Israelite—the last Adam was from heaven (God) in order to include both Gentiles and Israelites.*

The Apostle Paul explains Jesus's work as the last Adam:

> For as in Adam all die, so in Christ all will be made alive … So it is written: "The first man Adam became a living being" the last Adam, a life-giving spirit. (1 Corinthians 15:22, 45 NIV).

Paul the great apostle of grace had the revelation of Jesus's work as the last Adam. He understood that Jesus came to save the whole world. He understood that "all" (Israelites and Gentiles) were in him as he died and rose again from the dead. Jesus came to include Gentiles in God's eternal plan of sharing his life with the human race. He included them because it pleased God to have one family. In God's family, there is no Jew or Gentile because they are "all" one in Christ (Galatians 3:24–28). This is the good news, beloved! This is God's amazing grace, my friend!

Gentiles are not brought near God by the Law of Moses but by the blood of Christ. As we saw in the previous paragraphs, Jesus included Gentiles in his salvation—even if the Israelites segregated them because of the Law.

> But now in Christ Jesus you who once were far away have been brought near through the blood of Christ. (Ephesians 2:13 NIV)

What the Law of Moses could not accomplish, the blood of Jesus accomplished. Remember that the Gentiles were without Christ, separated with the nation of Israel, strangers from the Israelites' covenants and promises. They were in the world without God, but because of Christ's blood, they were brought near God. It was not because of the Law, but because of God's love and grace. That is why Christians have no relationship to the Mosaic Law whatsoever. We only rely on Jesus's finished work and his blood in our relationship with God.

By the cross, Jesus destroyed (put to death) the barrier of hostility and division between Gentiles and Israelites.

Paul continues by explaining that the wall of hostility between Gentiles and Israelites was destroyed or put to death by Jesus's cross. By the cross, Jesus reconciled Gentiles and Israelites to God. In his body (flesh), Jesus *abolished* the law with its commandments and regulations and created one new man out of the two (Gentiles and Israelites).

This truth is too good to be true for some believers, but that is the truth that will set you free. You have to appropriate it and walk in it. *There is no longer any difference between Gentiles and Israelites. We are one in Christ.* We are not under commandments or regulations as the Israelites were. That is why it is strange whenever I visit certain countries (especially in Europe and America) and see the racial divisions in the churches.

You find that some people cannot attend certain churches because they are known as "African/black churches" or "white churches." Beloved, we are one in Christ. We no longer judge anybody according to the flesh (2 Corinthians 5:16). Our earthly cultures differ, but our heavenly (kingdom) culture is the same all over the world. We must be freed from racism in the church if we are to enjoy God's grace to the fullest. We cannot pretend to be preaching or propagating the gospel of grace when we are racists. Racists are still in bondage because they do not walk in love. This applies to those bound by tribalism, especially in Africa and Asia. *God's grace unites us in Christ as one body. There is no room for racism, division, or tribalism.*

> For he himself is our peace, who has made the two one and has destroyed the barrier, the dividing wall of hostility, by abolishing in his flesh the law with its commandments and regulations. His purpose was to create in himself one new man out of the two, thus making peace, and in this one body to reconcile both of them to God through the cross, by which he put to death their hostility. He came and preached peace to you who were far away and peace to those who were near. (Ephesians 2:14–17 NIV)

Gentiles and Israelites both have access by one Spirit to the Father through Jesus Christ.

Beloved, Gentiles and the Israelites are one because of Christ. It is Christ who came to put us together by his death and resurrection. In the Old Covenant, even proselytes (circumcised Jews) were considered unholy because of their origin. They even were allocated their place in the temple worship. But now, because of Jesus, that wall of division has been pulled down. Hallelujah! We all have access to God through Jesus Christ by the Holy Spirit. This was not possible in the Old Testament. That is why Jesus is the way to the Father. He is not "a" way, but he is "the" Way (the only and true way).

Read Ephesians 2:18 for yourself and see how God loves you. You no longer need mediators for God to receive you. You have direct access to the throne of grace because of Jesus and the Holy Spirit (Hebrews 4:16). What the Law never allowed Gentiles to do, Jesus has given it to us free of charge, my friend. It is by grace, beloved! It is by Jesus because grace is a person—and his name is Jesus!

> For through him *we both* have access to the Father by one Spirit. (Ephesians 2:18 NIV, Emphasis added)

Gentiles and Israelites are both members of the household of God. *Gentiles are no longer strangers and foreigners as they were considered under the Mosaic Law.*

> Consequently, you are no longer foreigners and aliens, but fellow citizens with God's people and members of God's household. (Ephesians 2:19 NIV)

As we read this verse, we have to remember that Paul is writing to the church at Ephesus, which was mainly made of Gentile believers. He reminds them that they were no longer foreigners and aliens as in the Old Covenant. He reminds them that they were fellow citizens with God's people (Israelites) and members of God's household or family.

If you are in Christ, you are no longer a Gentile or alien. Gentiles existed in the Old Covenant. In the New Covenant, we have one family or the body of Christ, which is the assembly of the chosen or the *Ekklesia*.

Some preachers teach that believers are still under the Mosaic Law and that we must literally follow it. If that were the case, why don't we offer sacrifices for our sins? Why don't we have a physical temple and a high priest who would annually offer sacrifices on our behalf? Those teachers have a zeal for the things of God—but not according to knowledge. What knowledge am I talking about? It is the knowledge of the finished work of Christ. They are the ones who instill a sense of alienation from God in some believers who are not established in the finished work of Christ. No wonder many believers around the world consider themselves foreigners when the Bible calls them God's people (children) and members of God's household (family). If you are in that category, I pray that you receive this truth and walk in the freedom that Jesus gives free of charge.

We have to rightly divide the Word of God. We must diligently study and shamelessly teach what Jesus did once and for all for the human race. We must be teachable if we are to teach others. We must be Christ-centered and grace-oriented in our messages as ministers of the Spirit, but not of the letter. Remember that the letter (the Law) kills, but the Spirit gives life (2 Corinthians 3:6–9 NIV).

Gentiles are considered branches of a wild olive tree grafted into Jesus Christ because of their faith to share with the Israelites the richness of life promised in him.

> But if some of the branches were broken off, while you, a wild olive shoot, were grafted in among them to share the richness [of the root and sap] of the olive tree, do not boast over the branches and pride yourself at their expense. If you do boast and feel superior, remember it is not you that support the root, but the root [that supports] you. You will say then; Branches were broken (pruned) off so that I might be grafted in! That is true. But they were broken (pruned) off because of their unbelief (their lack of real faith), and you are established through faith [because you do believe]. So do not become proud and conceited, but rather stand in awe and be reverently afraid, (Romans 11:17–20 The Amplified Bible)

This verse is very clear and straightforward when talking about the Gentiles' place in relation to the Israelites and God's covenants.

We see that Paul calls the Gentiles "wild olive" to show that they were not part of the "branches" or the Israelites who are part of "the true olive" or Jesus as we can see in Ephesians

2:11–14. Paul goes on to remind them (Gentiles) that they do not have any reason for being proud and conceited because they were established or "grafted in" because of their faith. He reminded them that it was a gift from God—but not because they worked for it or deserved it.

Why did Paul have to remind them about this truth? It was because some of the Gentiles were being proud and belittling the Israelites by saying that they were better than them and that Israel would never be saved. Paul used this analogy to remind them that they were included in Christ because of his love and grace—but not because of their good works or merit. He wanted them to know that God is not yet done with Israel because Israelites shall be saved despite their current unbelief.

I have heard some preachers and believers contending that the church is the new Israel. To my knowledge, that is nowhere found in Scripture. *The church is not Israel, and she has not replaced Israel.* They are two different entities. What has changed is their place in God's covenants and promises. In the Old Testament, all the promises, the Law, the glory, the patriarchs, and the covenants belonged to the Israelites alone (Romans 9:1–5). But in the New Testament, because of Christ, we all belong to the body of Christ despite our physical differences (1 Corinthians 10:32). *We share whatever God has invested in Christ!*

Paul and the Gentiles

I cannot write on this topic without mentioning how Paul viewed the Gentiles in relation to the finished work of Christ. Paul testified to have been called to take the gospel of grace to the Gentiles or nations. This implies that his primary calling was to take Christ to non-Israelites.

> And the Lord said to me, Go, for I will send you far away unto the Gentiles (nations). (Acts 22:21 The Amplified Bible)

> But the Lord said to him, Go, for this man is a chosen instrument of Mine to bear My name before the Gentiles and kings and the descendants of Israel; For I will make clear to him how much he will be afflicted and must endure and suffer for My name's sake. (Acts 9:15 The Amplified Bible)

Paul and Barnabas were commissioned by the Holy Spirit to take the gospel of grace (Christ without the literal Law of Moses) to the Gentiles.

> In the church at Antioch there were prophets and teachers: Barnabas, Simeon called Niger, Lucius of Cyrene, Manaen (who had been brought up with Herod the tetrarch) and Saul. While they were

worshiping the Lord and fasting, *the Holy Spirit said, "Set apart for me Barnabas and Saul for the work to which I have called them."* So after they had fasted and prayed, they placed their hands on them and sent them off" (Acts: 1–2, NIV. Emphasis added).

Paul says that he was sent to the Gentiles (the uncircumcised) and Peter to the Israelites (the circumcised).

But on the contrary, when they [really] saw that *I had been entrusted [to carry] the Gospel to the uncircumcised [Gentiles,* just as definitely] as *Peter had been entrusted [to proclaim] the Gospel to the circumcised Jews,* [they were agreeable]; For He Who motivated *and* fitted Peter *and* worked effectively through him for the mission to the circumcised, motivated *and* fitted me *and* worked through me also for [the mission to] the Gentiles. (Galatians 2:7–8 The Amplified Bible. Emphasis added.)

Did Paul and Peter teach two different gospels? No! They preached the same gospel to two different audiences. To the Jews, Peter emphasized how all their promises were fulfilled in Christ. He explained that he was born under the Law to free them from the curse of the Law (Galatians 4:4).

On the other side, Paul taught the Gentiles that they were alienated from God, Christ, the covenants, all the promises, the glory, and the patriarchs (Romans 9:1–5). He reminded them that they were included in Christ before the foundation of the world (Ephesians 1:3–4, 2 Timothy 1:8–11). He told them that they had no relationship whatsoever to the Law—and that they only needed to believe Jesus Christ for their salvation. When dealing with a Jewish audience, Paul taught them as a people who knew the Law. When he had a Gentile audience, he spoke to them as people who never had any relationship with the Law of Moses.

Beloved, this is why understanding this truth is very fundamental to your Christian walk. If you are a teacher or preacher, you have to rightly divide the Word of God. *You have to know that the Law has never been given to the Gentiles.* Preach Christ and how he was crucified, rose from the dead, and is seated at the right hand of God with those who believe in him (Ephesians 2:6, Colossians 3:1–4). Jesus is our life!

Paul says that Gentiles are now to be fellow heirs with the Jews—members of the same body and joint partakers [sharing] in the same divine promise in Christ through their acceptance of the glad tidings (the gospel).

> For this reason, [because I preached that you are thus built up together], I, Paul, [am] the prisoner of Jesus the Christ for the sake and on behalf of you Gentiles— Assuming that you have heard of the stewardship of God's grace (his unmerited favor)

that was entrusted to me [to dispense to you] for your benefit, and] that the mystery (secret) was made known to me and I was allowed to comprehend it by direct revelation, as I already briefly wrote you. When you read this you can understand my insight into the mystery of Christ. [This mystery] was never disclosed to human beings in past generations as it has now been revealed to his holy apostles (consecrated messengers) and prophets by the [Holy] Spirit. [It is this:] that the Gentiles are now to be fellow heirs [with the Jews], members of the same body and joint partakers [sharing] in the same divine promise in Christ through [their acceptance of] the glad tidings (the Gospel). Of this [Gospel] I was made a minister according to the gift of God's free grace (undeserved favor) which was bestowed on me by the exercise (the working in all its effectiveness) of his power. (Ephesians 3:1–7 The Amplified Bible. Emphasis added).

Paul continually testifies that Gentiles and Israelites (Jews) are *now* fellow heirs, members of the same body (the church or the same body), and joint partakers in the same divine promise in Christ through their acceptance of the gospel or good news. Paul calls this "the mystery of Christ," which was hidden for ages. It was not disclosed to human beings in past generations. It was *revealed* (or made known by special knowledge from the Holy Spirit) to God's holy apostles and prophets.

Beloved, that is why the church must come back to this vital truth that the early church dearly preached. *We must come back to the true gospel.*

I pray that this divine revelation becomes your revelation now. I pray that you will walk in this truth and be freed from any religious mind-set that is haunting you. Beloved, I suggest you take a short pause and thank God for having come in the person of Christ to include you in his eternal plan. Before you continue with your reading, take some time to whisper to him how grateful you are for his love, grace, and mercy toward you!

Peter and the Gentiles

In the previous paragraphs, we saw how the apostle Paul related with the Gentiles and the Law. When dealing with a Gentile audience, he spoke to them as a people who had never had any relationship with the Law. He presented Christ to them without putting them under the Law of Moses. When dealing with an Israelite (Jewish) audience, he taught them as a people who were under the Law—but they needed Jesus who had come to set them free from the curse of the

Law (Galatians 3:10–13). Let's see how Peter related to the Gentiles.

Even after Jesus' ascension to Heaven, Peter still considered the Gentiles to be unholy and unclean as the Law said and discriminated them.

> The next day as they were still on their way and were approaching the town, Peter went up to the roof of the house to pray, about the sixth hour (noon). But he became very hungry, and wanted something to eat; and while the meal was being prepared a trance came over him,
>
> And he saw the sky opened and something like a great sheet lowered by the four corners, descending to the earth. It contained all kinds of quadrupeds and wild beasts and creeping things of the earth and birds of the air. And there came a voice to him, saying, rise up, Peter, kill and eat.
>
> But Peter said, No, by no means, Lord; for I have never eaten anything that is common and unhallowed or [ceremonially] unclean.
>
> And the voice came to him again a second time, What God has cleansed and pronounced clean, do not you defile and profane by regarding and calling common and unhallowed or unclean.

This occurred three times; then immediately the sheet was taken up to heaven. Now Peter was still inwardly perplexed and doubted as to what the vision which he had seen could mean, when [just then] behold the messengers that were sent by Cornelius, who had made inquiry for Simon's house, stopped and stood before the gate ... As Peter arrived, Cornelius met him, and falling down at his feet he made obeisance and paid worshipful reverence to him. But Peter raised him up, saying, Get up; I myself am also a man.

And as [Peter] spoke with him, he entered the house and found a large group of persons assembled; And he said to them, You yourselves are aware how it is not lawful or permissible for a Jew to keep company with or to visit or [even] to come near or to speak first to anyone of another nationality, but God has shown and taught me by words that I should not call any human being common or unhallowed or [ceremonially] unclean. (Acts 10:9–17, 25–28 The Amplified Bible)

It has always amazed me that Peter lived with Jesus but could not understand that God had a plan of saving the Gentiles in Christ. Did Jesus ever teach the apostles how in him Gentiles were going to be saved? Did Peter understand what Jesus taught on this subject? These questions are not easy to answer, but after Pentecost, Peter still believed that Gentiles were ceremonially unclean and unholy. Because of that understanding, he viewed them as not qualified to take part in the Holy Spirit.

In the above passage, Peter got a vision from the Lord Jesus and refused to accept it because it did not align with what he believed. He still considered the Gentiles unholy and unclean.

According to the Jewish culture, it was not lawful or permissible for a Jew to keep company with, visit, go near, or speak first to anyone of another nationality. The Jews considered other people unclean and unholy. As a devout Jew, Peter still believed it and could not relate with any Gentile. God had to break through his religious mind-set by making him understand that he should not consider any human being unholy or unclean because all races were included in Jesus who is the last Adam (1 Corinthians 15:22, 45). Peter repented (changed his mind) and took the good news to Cornelius and his household.

One of the things that God uses in teaching us his purposes is challenging our understanding. Peter thought he knew it all because he had walked with Jesus, but to his amazement, he still had a lot to learn about God's grace and mercy.

As Peter started sharing with Cornelius and other people with him, he made the confession of his life.

> I now realize how true it is that God does not show
> favoritism, but accepts men from every nation who
> fear him and do what is right. (Acts 10:34–35, NIV)

God wanted Peter and other Jews with him to know that
God loves and accepts the whole world. He does not show
favoritism as the Israelites thought God did. He had come to
love the whole world in Christ. God proved that by giving
the Holy Spirit to the Gentiles in the same way the Jews had
received him. After that mind-changing event, Luke narrates
what happens next in these piercing words:

> While Peter was still speaking these words, the
> Holy Spirit came on all who heard the message.
> The circumcised believers who had come with
> Peter were astonished that the gift of the Holy
> Spirit had been poured out even on the Gentiles.
> For they heard them speaking in tongues and
> praising God. Then Peter said, "Can anyone keep
> these people from being baptized with water? They
> have received the Holy Spirit just as we have. So he
> ordered that they be baptized in the name of Jesus
> Christ. Then they asked Peter to stay with them
> for a few days." (Acts 10:44–48 NIV)

This event was the beginning of a great shift in the early
church. Jews who thought salvation was exclusively for the

nation of Israel were amazed to see that even Gentiles could receive the Holy Spirit and speak in tongues. This is the mystery of the church. It includes both Jews and Gentiles because of Christ's finished work.

Paul opposed Peter because he was forcing Gentiles to follow Jewish customs.

If there is a person who had the revelation of Jesus's finished work, it was Paul. *Paul was a radical grace preacher and teacher.* He was not afraid to challenge and oppose Peter the great apostle of the early church when he walked in hypocrisy.

Jewish customs segregated the Gentiles. They would not share a meal with them even when they wanted to. Most of the early church believers still viewed Gentiles as unholy and unclean. They considered them second-class citizens.

Paul fervently opposed Peter in front of others because he was living in hypocrisy. Before men from James came to Antioch, Peter shared his meal with Gentiles without any problem. Because he was afraid of the apostle James who was Jesus's brother (Galatians 1:19) and the apostle of the church of Jerusalem, he withdrew and refused to continue eating with them. Without any hesitation, Paul publicly opposed him.

When Peter came to Antioch, I opposed him to his face, because he was clearly in the wrong. Before certain men came from James, he used to eat with the Gentiles. But when they arrived, he began to draw back and separate himself from the Gentiles because he was afraid of those who belonged to the circumcision group. The other Jews joined him in his hypocrisy, so that by their hypocrisy even Barnabas was led astray. When I saw that they were not acting in line with the truth of the gospel, I said to Peter in front of them all, "You are a Jew, yet you live like a Gentile and not like a Jew. How is it, then, that you force Gentiles to follow Jewish customs? "We who are Jews by birth and not 'Gentile sinners' know that a man is not justified by observing the law, but by faith in Jesus Christ. So we, too, have put our faith in Christ Jesus that we may be justified by faith in Christ and not by observing the law, because by observing the law no one will be justified." (Galatians 2:11–16 NIV)

Jews separated themselves from Gentiles because they considered them sinners by birth. For that reason, they were unholy and unclean (according to the Law of Moses). Peter had understood that Gentiles were also included in Christ, but he was afraid of those who belonged to the circumcision group.

The circumcision group was a sect that defended circumcision as a vital qualification for being eligible for salvation. For them, no one could be saved unless they were circumcised. They contended that justification by faith was not enough. People still needed some portions of the Law in order to be part of the church. They wanted Gentiles to be physically like them in order to fellowship with them. That was why Paul had to publicly oppose Peter. He was not acting in line with the truth of the gospel and was forcing Gentiles to follow Jewish customs.

What does the truth of the gospel say? It says that Jews and Gentiles who believe in Christ are one body. It says that we share all the promises found in Christ. It says that we are all justified by faith in Jesus Christ. *We* don't need circumcision to be saved, but we need to *only* believe and receive the abundance of grace and the free gift of righteousness (Romans 5:17). The consequence to that is reigning in life together (Jews and Gentiles) in life through Jesus Christ.

The Jerusalem Council

One of the most important meetings that the early church had is known as the "Jerusalem Council." In this meeting, the apostles and elders sat together to study how Gentiles were to be taught and considered in the church. Were they going to be under the Law of Moses or under faith? Were they going to be rejected or accepted? Let's see why the meeting took place and its resolutions.

Controversy arises within the church

> Certain people came down from Judea to Antioch and were teaching the brothers: Unless you are circumcised, according to the custom taught by Moses, you cannot be saved. (Acts 15:1 NIV)

These men were teaching that circumcision was required for salvation. Their thinking went this way: "How can one be saved and belong unless he is circumcised as our Patriarch Abraham did? Even Moses the great lawgiver commanded us to be circumcised as a physical sign proving that we belong to God and obey him. These men want an easy life. No way! They must be circumcised or else we will not accept them (Genesis 17:12)."

Paul and Barnabas go to Jerusalem

This brought Paul and Barnabas into sharp dispute and debate with them. Paul and Barnabas were appointed, along with some other believers, to go up to Jerusalem to see the apostles and elders about this question. The church sent them on their way, and as they traveled through Phoenicia and Samaria, they told how the Gentiles had been converted.

This news made all the brothers very glad. When they came to Jerusalem, they were welcomed by the church and the apostles and elders—to whom they reported everything God—had done through them.

> Then some of the believers who belonged to the party of the Pharisees stood up and said, "The Gentiles must be circumcised and required to obey the Law of Moses." (Acts 15:2–5 NIV)

As we earlier saw, Paul and Barnabas were set apart by the Holy Spirit to take the gospel to the Gentiles. They had experienced how God saved them and healed them by the power of the Holy Spirit. However, some people of the party of the Pharisees who had believed in Christ still held strongly to the fact that Gentiles had to be required to obey the Law of Moses. To them, salvation equaled Jesus plus the Law of Moses or nothing at all. For them, giving up on the Law was giving up on God. How could anybody be a partaker of the Abrahamic blessing unless they were circumcised? According to members of that sect, that was utter foolishness. So, because of this dispute within the church, Paul and Barnabas were sent to Jerusalem to consult with the apostles and elders.

I like the way Paul and Barnabas had to consult the apostles and elders. They learned what leadership meant within the church. They had to report to those who were leading that great reformation.

It is sad that the current church no longer solves doctrinal differences this way. Whenever a misunderstanding arises within the church, some are chased away and rejected instead of meeting and amicably resolving the problems in the light of the truth of the gospel of Jesus Christ. I know that sometimes it is not easy because most church leaders don't really understand the finished work of Jesus, but a compromise can still be found when people are acting in love.

> The apostles and elders met to consider this question. After much discussion, Peter got up and addressed them: "Brothers, you know that some time ago God made a choice among you that the Gentiles might hear from my lips the message of the gospel and believe. God, who knows the heart, showed that he accepted them by giving the Holy Spirit to them, just as he did to us. He made no distinction between us and them, for he purified their hearts by faith. Now then, why do you try to test God by putting on the necks of the disciples a yoke that neither we nor our fathers have been able to bear? No! We believe it is through the grace of our Lord Jesus that we are saved, just as they are."
> The whole assembly became silent as they listened

> to Barnabas and Paul telling about the miraculous
> signs and wonders God had done among the
> Gentiles through them. (Acts 15:6–12 NIV)

As I read this passage, I traveled back in time. I went to
that meeting and witnessed how it was tense. I could see
members of the circumcision group and the Pharisees
arguing that salvation is obtained by literally following the
Law of Moses. I could see them saying that Gentiles who are
not circumcised are not yet saved. On the other side, I could
see Paul and Barnabas fervently arguing that Gentiles are
saved by grace through faith in Jesus Christ as Peter testifies
in Acts 15:11. The meeting was very heated!

Peter stood and reminded them of the event we saw
in Acts 10. He talked about how God chose him to take
the gospel to the Gentiles and how they received the Holy
Spirit just like they did. He reminded them that the Gentiles'
hearts were purified by faith and saved by grace just like
them. Paul and Barnabas supported his argument by giving
testimonies about how God performed many miraculous
signs and wonders among Gentiles through them.

> He made no distinction between us and them, for
> he purified their hearts by faith. Now then, why
> do you try to test God by putting on the necks of
> the disciples a yoke that neither we nor our fathers

have been able to bear? No! We believe it is through the grace of our Lord Jesus that we are saved, just as they are. (Acts 15:9–11 NIV)

I have heard some teachers say that Peter did not have a revelation about the grace of God, but this statement shows that he understood what God had done in Christ and how Gentiles were to be considered in the light of the Gospel. He contended that, because of Christ, there was no distinction between Israelites and Gentiles because they were both purified in their hearts by their faith in Jesus. Peter could not understand why the members of the circumcision group wanted to put on the necks of the disciples a yoke that neither they (the Israelites of the time) nor their fathers had been able to bear. In Jeremiah 31:31–34, God says that the Israelites violated the Covenant of the Law; that was why he was going to make a New Covenant with the tribe of Judah (but not with the tribe of Levi). *That is why the New Covenant is by faith, but not by works of the Law. God ushered it in so that Gentiles would be qualified by their faith in Jesus, but not by the Mosaic Law since they had never been under it.*

We must believe that we are saved through the grace of our Lord Jesus. That truth applies to the Gentiles and the Israelites. Michael Morrison clarifies this truth by saying,

Today, we might explain that Jesus instituted a new covenant, and that the Jewish believers were God's people not because they were Jewish, but because they were believers. Membership in the new covenant is by faith, not by ancestry. Salvation is by grace through faith for whoever calls upon the name of Jesus Christ. (Ephesians 2:8–9, Romans 10:9–11)

When they finished, James spoke up: "Brothers, listen to me. Simon has described to us how God at first showed his concern by taking from the Gentiles a people for himself. The words of the prophets are in agreement with this, as it is written: after this I will return and rebuild David's fallen tent. Its ruins I will rebuild, and I will restore it, that the remnant of men may seek the Lord, and all the Gentiles who bear my name, says the Lord, who does these things that have been known for ages. "It is my judgment, therefore, that we should not make it difficult for the Gentiles who are turning to God. Instead we should write to them, telling them to abstain from food polluted by idols, from sexual immorality, from the meat of strangled animals and from blood. For Moses has been preached in every city from the earliest times and is read in the synagogues on every Sabbath. (Acts 15:13–21 NIV)

James was a leader in the church of Jerusalem and provided many solutions. He was also a respected apostle who had many followers. He was not legalistic as many people teach; he was in total agreement with Paul and Peter as we can see in that portion of scripture. Michael Morrison once again explains this truth:

> After Barnabas and Paul told "about the signs and wonders God had done among the Gentiles" (Acts 15:12), James spoke. As leader of the Jerusalem church, he had a lot of influence. Some of the Judaizers even claimed him as their authority (Galatians 2:12), but Luke tells us that James was in complete agreement with Peter and Paul.

As we can see, James was in total agreement with Paul and Peter, but some of his followers did not understand that Gentiles were saved by faith in Christ, but not by circumcision or any other work of the Law. He reminded them that the words of the prophets were in total agreement with what Peter did (Acts 15:15). It was not an issue of Jewish tradition; it was a dispute about the Law. No one in Israel was obliged to follow other traditions rather than those written in the book of Moses.

Instead we should write to them, telling them to abstain from food polluted by idols, from sexual immorality, from the meat of strangled animals and from blood. (Acts 15:20 NIV)

James proposed four solutions:

- abstaining from food polluted by animals
- abstaining from sexual immorality
- abstaining from strangled animals
- abstaining from blood

Why give them these four rules? Michael Morrison has an answer.

We "should not make it difficult for the Gentiles, James said. Instead, it will be enough to give them four rules, which they will find easy to comply with. Why give them these rules? Notice the reason that James gives: 'For the law of Moses has been preached in every city from the earliest times and is read in the synagogues on every Sabbath.'" (v. 21) James was not encouraging Gentile Christians to attend the synagogues. He was not saying they should listen to the laws of Moses. No, but because those laws were commonly preached, the apostles should tell the Gentiles four rules. Then they would not think that Christianity is more difficult than it is.

The Apostles' Letter to Gentile Believers

> The apostles and elders, your brothers, To the Gentile believers in Antioch, Syria and Cilicia: Greetings. We have heard that some went out from us without our authorization and disturbed you, troubling your minds by what they said. So we all agreed to choose some men and send them to you with our dear friends Barnabas and Paul— men who have risked their lives for the name of our Lord Jesus Christ. Therefore, we are sending Judas and Silas to confirm by word of mouth what we are writing. It seemed good to the Holy Spirit and to us not to burden you with anything beyond the following requirements: You are to abstain from food sacrificed to idols, from blood, from the meat of strangled animals and from sexual immorality. You will do well to avoid these things. (Acts 15:23–29 NIV)

After James's speech, the apostles, elders, and other brothers at the meeting decided to send a letter to the Gentile believers. The introduction of the letter looks like an apology directed to them because of what some brethren (those from the circumcision group) did. They said the brethren had disturbed and troubled their minds by what they said. Because of that, the apostles, elders, brothers, and the Holy Spirit were pleased "not to burden" them beyond the four rules previously mentioned. What had they said? They had forced Gentiles to go back to the Law of Moses. They had required them to be circumcised when they had never been under the Law of Moses.

This kind of teaching is still prevalent in churches around the world. I have heard many "famous" preachers contend that Christians (especially Gentile believers) are under the Law. Some even quote to prove their point when teaching about prosperity and success in life.

As born again believers, we no longer meditate on the Law of Moses in order to be successful. No! We meditate on Jesus Christ and his finished work. We live by faith and follow the leading of the Holy Spirit. The New Covenant encourages us to be filled of the Holy Spirit because he Is the One who leads us into success. (Joshua 1:8–9)

It also encourages us to be full of the Word of Christ (Colossians 3:16, Ephesians 5:18). Those who say that they meditate on the Law of Moses still need to get a revelation of the finished work of Jesus Christ. We are no longer under the Law, beloved. We are under grace, and under grace, God has already blessed us. We live from a place of blessedness (Romans 6:14, Ephesians 1:3). You are blessed, my friend! Confess it out loud. Receive it, believe it, and live it because it is your heritage in Christ.

My prayer is that God will raise a new generation of grace teachers and preachers. These people will love the body of Christ (the church) because they have understood that they are highly favored and deeply loved in Christ. I pray that these men and women will rise up in this dying world as a great army of the kingdom of God. I pray that, as you study through these lines, the Holy Spirit will reveal Christ to your heart so that you may walk in grace and truth found in Jesus (John 1:16–17).

Beloved, if you are a Gentile believer, you have never been under the Law of Moses. You were born into grace. You are under grace. Does it mean that we disregard the Law or the Old Testament? No! To the contrary, we establish the Law or testify what it says to be true (Romans 3:31).

When we read or study the Old Testament, we have to be aware that it talks about Jesus Christ and his mission. That is why we don't disregard it or throw it away just because we are in the New Testament or under grace (Luke 24:24–45).

The Law of Moses required total and eternal righteousness. Jesus came to fulfill or accomplish that need. The Law, as we saw, was never given to Gentiles. It was exclusively for the nation of Israel as its constitution. It clarified how Gentiles were to be treated, especially those living in Israel. It also clarified how Gentiles were going to be included in the church without the Law of Moses.

Because of Christ, Gentiles and Israelites form one body. In the New Covenant, we are not allowed to go back to the Law of Moses and live by it because we live by the Law of the Spirit of life in Christ (Romans 8:1–4). It is not the Law of Moses, but the Law of the Spirit of life in Christ.

Remember that the Law kills, but the Spirit gives life (2 Corinthians 3:6–9). Jesus said that if we abide in his teachings, we shall know the truth—and the truth shall set us free. The truth is not a set of beliefs or doctrines. The truth is the person of Jesus (John 8:31–36, John 14:6, John 3:36). When you know Jesus, you will never again walk in darkness. May you live in the grace, love, and freedom that God has given us in Jesus Christ (Galatians 5:1).

Prayer of Thanksgiving

Before putting down this book: I want us to pray together as we thank the Lord Jesus for his grace and Love:

> Heavenly Father, in the name of Jesus, I thank you for your grace and love. I thank you because you thought about me before the creation of the

world. That is amazing and mind-blowing. I thank you because I am not under the Law, but under grace. Thank you because you have revealed to me through this book that Gentiles have never and will never be under the Law. They are under faith just as Abraham was. He lived before the Law and related with you in faith. Thank you for your gift of faith. I love you, Father. Thank you for Jesus. I want to know him more and more and get to know you through him. I bless you and worship you. In Jesus's name, I pray. Amen!

BIBLIOGRAPHY

1. Mad. Claudia R Wintoch and Tom Trout., "The inclusion of Gentiles in the Old Testament", Old Testament Theology, World Revival School Ministry. Spring Trimester 2003, last accessed December 15,2016, http://healing2thenations.net/papers/gentiles.htm.

2. "Exclusion of Gentiles in the Old Testament", last accessed December 15,2016, http:// www. rationalchristianity. Net

3. "To what Law were the Ancient Gentiles accountable?", last accessed December 15, 2016, http://www. christiancourier. Com

4. "Exploring the book of Acts 15. Up decree of the council of Jerusalem (Acts 15) Part 1: the literary flow of Acts 15", Last Accessed December 15,2016, http:// www. gci. Org

5. "Scripture taken from *The Message.* Copyright © 1993, 1994, 1995, 1996, 2000, 2001, 2002. Used by permission of NavPress Publishing Group."

6. Hebrew-Greek Key Word Study Bible. Copyright c 1996 by AMG International, Inc.

7. New International Bible Dictionary. Based on the NIV/Edition 1, J. D Douglas, John R. Kohlenberger III, EdwardW. Good rick. Zondervan (www. Zondervan. com).

8. "A list of the 613 Mitzvot (commandments)", © Copyright 5757-5771 (1996-2011), Tracey R Rich, last accessed December 15,2016, http://www.jewfaq.org

9. THE HOLY BIBLE, NEW INTERNATIONAL VERSION®, NIV® Copyright © 1973, 1978, 1984, 2011 by Biblica, Inc. ® Used by permission. All rights reserved worldwide.

10. "Scripture quotations taken from the Amplified® Bible (AMP), Copyright © 2015 by The Lockman Foundation, last accessed December 15,2016, Used by permission. www. Lockman. org"

11. Scriptures marked KJV are taken from the KING JAMES VERSION (KJV), public domain, last accessed

December 1, 2016, https://www.biblegateway.com/versions/King-James-Version-KJV-Bible/

12. Matthew George Easton, The Easton's Bible Dictionary Online, last accessed December 15,2016, http://www.biblestudytools.com/,Thomas Nelson, 1897.

Printed in the United States
By Bookmasters